IT IS POSSIBLE...
BELIEVE!

By

Evans Ogboi

DEDICATION

For /that special person
trying to navigate through life's battles,
and searching for answers... may you find them

For that person looking for purpose...
may you discover it.

There is unimaginable potential; a world of possibilities
unravelled only for the one who believes.

TABLE OF CONTENTS

FOREWORD

It Is Possible, If You Know What It Is!

The things that get us into trouble, make us prone to mistakes, push us into presumptuousness, eventually paralyse us and cause us to experience perennial discouragement are those things we know *generally*, and not *specifically*.

If I ask an average Christian what his future is like, he will say without hesitation: "I have a great future!" Some would even say: "*my future* is so bright, you'll have to wear sunglasses when you look at it!"

These responses make great Instagram post captions, but once you request for *specific details* of what this expected future is anchored on, the responses fall apart.

This is precisely where the enemy wins. He said to Eve, "has God said?"

Optimism is not faith, because anyone could stay positive, and wish themselves well, and we should.

But look at the Apostle Paul:

For this reason, I also suffer these things; nevertheless, I am not ashamed, for I know whom I have believed and am persuaded that He is able to keep what I have committed to Him until that Day. - **2 Timothy 1:12 NKJV**

And again,

For I am persuaded that neither death nor life, nor angels nor principalities nor powers, nor things present nor things to come, nor height nor depth, nor any other created thing, shall be able to separate us from the love of God which is in Christ Jesus our Lord. - **Romans 8:38-39 NKJV**

We confess these scriptures; but these are Paul's personal persuasions, not ours.

How do you know? Well, he told us to pray for ours in Ephesians 3, from verse 14. The result of this prayer and communion will then be:

Then you will be empowered to discover what every holy one experiences—the great magnitude of the astonishing love of Christ in all its dimensions. How deeply intimate and far-reaching is his love! How enduring and inclusive it is! Endless love beyond measurement that transcends our understanding— this extravagant love pours into you until you are filled to overflowing with the fullness of God! - **Ephesians 3:18-19 TPT**

I love how he emphasizes that this experience is guaranteed for ALL SAINTS, this capacity to perceive God's love BY REVELATION KNOWLEDGE.

Your future is not deciphered from head knowledge or quoting a handful of scriptures by heart, but must be *vivid and real to your spirit*, and anchored in the love of God. It must be unshakable, persuasive, pervasive and expansive enough, that no devil in hell with their lying wonders can dissuade you!

The REVELATION is waiting on your entering into God's presence to secure it.

> *I pray that the light of God will illuminate the eyes of your imagination, flooding you with light, until you experience the full revelation of the hope of his calling—that is, the wealth of God's glorious inheritances that he finds in us, his holy ones! -* ***Ephesians 1:18 TPT***

This is the foundation of your confidence. This is our altar. Our daily cultivation, communion and worship to the Father; this is the point of contact of power.

Read the next verse:

> *I pray that you will continually experience the immeasurable greatness of God's power made available to you through faith. Then your lives will be an advertisement of this immense power as it works through you! This is the mighty power - **Ephesians 1:19 TPT***

Paul is saying that the revealed will of God for our lives (the hope of His calling) is the entrance of the resurrection power of God – through our fellowship with the Father on the platform of His purposes and plans, we experience His power constantly, the power that causes us to fulfil this great calling.

No focus, no power!

Worship and joy will trigger our imagination in line with His purposes and plans. We will begin to have inspired imageries based on these plans, images inspired by the Holy Spirit to build our faith and edify us on our journeys.

Optimism is good, but it is rooted in human senses, and will fall like pack of cards at the sight of the first headwind. On the flipside, God's hope is an anchor for the soul, hooked to the Mercy Seat (the love of God in Christ Jesus, our Lord).

> *We have this certain hope like a strong, unbreakable anchor holding our souls to God himself. Our anchor of hope is fastened to the mercy seat which sits in the heavenly realm beyond the sacred threshold,* **- Hebrews 6:19 TPT**

Everything I have described thus far is part of what the scriptures refer to as: *seeking and seeing the kingdom of God.* This is a commandment of grace. Yes, grace has commandments too.

Once this begins to settle in you and the light of God's Spirit begins to bloom in you, you will begin to see beyond where you are, what you're doing, what you currently have; you will begin to see into the future God has prepared.

You will begin to walk into God's glory for you.
You will begin to see that IT IS indeed POSSIBLE!

Evans has written a guide, a handbook so precise and practical, one authenticated by a soul that has lived the truths I described above – practically and truthfully.

It is indeed my honour to write these few words because I have met the man, and I have witnessed his journey. He is not a hustler trying to make a buck, but a purposeful minister who has and will indeed make a mark in his calling and for his generation.

The pages of this book will inspire you, ground you, prepare you and light the fire of truth inside you, so you can escape the corruption of frivolities and pursue a destiny already substantiated by your Father in Christ Jesus. It is a tested treatise of faith, from one who carried his gift on the back seats of Lagos "okadas", going from studio to studio, from stage to stage, but whose gift has begun to carry him.

It's possible, because IT IS FINISHED!

Femi Jacobs

INTRODUCTION

Beyond the Limits

22nd October 2014.
Wembley Arena, London.

Outside the Wembley Arena, top musical and entertainment personalities across the world strut the red carpet, dressed to the nines.

Pressed on the side-lines was a pulsating crowd of fans, reporters and entertainment enthusiasts, with bright smiles, hopeful to catch a glimpse of their favourite stars who had travelled across the world to grace one of Britain's biggest events – the MOBO awards.

The MOBOs, running since the mid 1990's, celebrated Music of Black Origin, and had become a pivotal event in Britain, recognising and awarding black excellence. The 2014 MOBOs was held in London, anchored by the talented and beautiful Sarah Jena Crawford and Mel B.

The evening progressed with musical acts gracing the lavish stage with performances, and heart-stopping moments when award nominees were called out, and the celebration and big reveal that followed when the winners were announced. Suddenly, it was the moment I had been waiting for.

"And the MOBO award goes for the Best Gospel Act goes to…" Mel B opened the envelope, "The Living Faith Choir…"

The applause that followed was deafening. A familiar song that suddenly seemed so strange began to play; the lyrics were perfect for what was currently unfolding.

Beyond the norm; beyond my fears
Beyond the natural, I will excel
I'm soaring high beyond the sky
By the power of the Lord!
Beyond the limits, beyond the norm
Beyond the ordinary – we overcome!
If God be for us, who can stand against us?
We have the victory through Christ the Lord!

I jumped to my feet, and walked through the crowd and the applause, following the hurried steps of Pastor Chris Adeoye, my mentor and Pastor of my church, *RCCG Living Faith Connections.*

All eyes were on us, and several cameras trailed our path as we quickly walked towards the podium to receive the award.

As we neared the podium, I hesitated. Pastor Chris instinctively turned to me and quickly gestured with his hand that I follow him, then he broke into a light race up the steps to the podium. I followed suite and bounded up the steps, after him.

And there it was – The 2014 MOBO award for best Gospel Act.

Incredible!

Living Faith Connection Choir, the choir I directed and worked with for days and nights, had just won an international award.

I stood there before the unbelievable crowd, my heart racing with excitement, overjoyed, and a feeling of accomplishment swept over me. I wondered several times over – *is this a dream?*

I was humbled by the weight of success, and the knowledge of a divine manifestation of God's grace and purpose. How exactly had a Nigerian boy of a humble background from Benin City, West Africa come to this point where his effort and labour was being celebrated by this lavish crowd, and honoured on a global scale by the very best in the music industry? In one single glimpse, my life flashed before me.

"This is the reward of hard work, to the glory of God…" As Pastor Chris gave the acceptance speech, I stood rooted, my hands clasped together, a smile spread across my face.

I had that feeling.

It was so overwhelming, but *we* did this. *We* made this happen!

Success is overwhelming. Bracing the tape is overwhelming.

When you achieve that goal, the feeling that overcomes you is sensational, but more overpowering is the truth that anything you desire is achievable!

What is your goal?

What is that one thing you desire so badly, you wonder if it can ever become a reality?

Are you seeking to clinch that gold medal? Birth an impossible dream? Marry the girl of your dreams? Throw your graduation cap to the blue skies? Break the ceiling of your career? Get a promotion at work? Nurse a dying business to flourishing health. Carry your long-awaited baby in your arms? Walk into a season of breakthrough? Repair a broken relationship?

Friends, I would like to announce to you, that whatever you seek to achieve, it is possible!

The ability to live your dreams lies within your reach, and in the next few pages of this book, I will be sharing with you, seven anchors to guide you from where you are to where you are meant to be – where God has destined you to be.

An anchor is a piece of metal that is used by sailors to secure a boat and keep it on a steady course. Without an anchor, a water vessel, no matter how big it is, would drift away from its destination, and get lost at sea.

When you are anchored in God's truth, you stay in course, and remain focused on the task to be done. And even through the winds of challenges, the storms of life and confusion, you remain focused, and fixed, overcome doubt, pressure, fear, and remain rooted and grounded.

Break out of limiting belief systems, shatter ceilings, reach for a life of possibilities, and unlock the greatness that God has deposited in you.

Evans Ogboi

"I serve a God who cannot lie
I believe all He says is true
With a word spoken over me
He has secured my destiny…"

Lyrics from Song: He's Able
Words & Music by Evans Ogboi
©2022 Simplicity Records

ANCHOR 1

FAITH

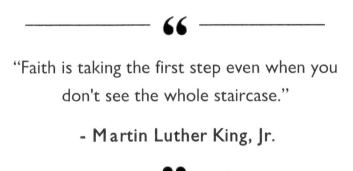

"Faith is taking the first step even when you don't see the whole staircase."

- Martin Luther King, Jr.

FAITH IN GOD

*"And without faith it is impossible to please Him, for he who comes to God must believe that He is and that He is a rewarder of those who seek Him." - **Hebrews 11:6***

Faith is the supernatural currency with which we trade with to receive heavenly realities on earth.

With faith, it is possible to access a heaven-on-earth lifestyle, and literally do the impossible.

Never ignore faith or take it lightly; faith helped me through my journey and is still taking me to greater heights.

The world we know today was created from the invisible realm, and it was framed by the word of God.

Hebrews 11 is a powerful chapter of Scripture and verses 1 and 2 says;

'Faith is the substance of things hoped for, the evidence of things not seen for by it the elders obtained a good report. Through faith, we understand that the worlds were framed by the word of God so that the things which are seen were not made of things which do appear'

There is a world of possibilities that exist when you believe.

Your very existence is a miracle!

The fact that you survived for weeks in your mother's womb, and nine months afterwards, you were born into the world is not only a miracle, but sustainable proof that there is a God in the invisible realm who orchestrates these miracles.

The Bible says in Hebrews 11 verse 6:

> *'But without faith, it is impossible to please Him, for he that cometh to God must believe that He is and that He is a rewarder of them, that diligently seek Him'.*

To experience this realm of miracles, you must believe in the existence of God; the One who is behind the scenes, working everything out for your good.

You were created for a purpose, and specifically born into your country of nativity, tribe, and family.

You have been spared for such a time as this for a purpose and God has a divine plan for your life. There are limitless possibilities that exist when you walk with God.

Notwithstanding your views and imaginations, or the circumstances you have been through – you can be anything and achieve anything! If you put your mind to it, you can unlock possibilities.

It is Possible!

No man walks with God except by faith because God's ways are not our ways. A mortal man cannot comprehend the things of God and so we walk by faith and not by sight.

Overall, accept in your heart that the invisible realm is real. Believe that there is a God that does exist and watches over your life and determine to be committed to a life of seeking to do the impossible!

ANCHORED ACTIONS

Think through these questions, to create your plan.

- God has orchestrated your life. List out some of the miracles you have experienced in your life.

- What are the things you are grateful to God for in your life? You might be facing challenges, but there is always a reason to be grateful!

POINT TO PONDER

Our lives are like a movie, where God is the script writer, producer, originator of the plan, and constructor of our journey; but we must live it all out by faith for us to experience endless possibilities.

DO YOU BELIEVE?

*"Therefore I tell you, whatever you ask for in prayer, believe that you have received it, and it will be yours." - **Mark 11:24***

It is commonly said that: *seeing is believing* but in God's Kingdom, you must believe the invisible to see it manifest in reality. This is the power of vision.

Vision is the ability to see and believe God's plan for your life as it unfolds, step by step. Irrespective of your background, culture, race, personality or present situation, do you believe in greatness?

I was born on the 23rd of June 1982 in the busy, commercial city of Lagos, in South-West Nigeria. As I grew into adolescence, I was literally wandering about the streets of Benin, without a direction or a clue to where I was going. I had lost all my friends, every sense of belonging, and at some point, I felt I was losing my mind.

It was in that state of confusion that God picked me up, showed me my purpose and where he wanted me to be; At a tender age, the Lord called me, and began to order my steps to do specific things; these were pointers that revealed the path to my destiny.

Today, by His grace, I have grown from that confused teenager in Benin City to a multi-award-winning gospel artiste who resides in the UK with his beautiful family, runs a record label, and creates music that spreads impact, touches the globe, and serves the music industry and larger community.

I am in the business of creating quality content for the Kingdom that is blessing lives across the globe. All this came to pass because I believed.

It starts from what you believe.

Do you believe?
Do you believe that you are special?
Do you believe that you have what it takes?
Do you believe that things are working in your favour?

- Do you believe that you can be all that God wants you to be? Do you believe that God has created you to be the best version of yourself?

- Do you believe that you are going somewhere great to manifest? Do you believe that God is counting on you to make a change, and to make a difference in your family?

- Do you believe that you have the solution that the world is seeking today?

- Do you believe that in you lies a seed of greatness that can stir up a series of events and certain moves that will transform the entire world?

- Do you believe it?

History has the records of men and women who unleashed their potential because they dared to believe. These men or women were not any better than you, they just believed that they had what it took to make a difference and they acted on their belief.

All things are possible to them that believe!

You must make up in your mind to not only believe that you are special, but to also believe that God has blessed you with everything that pertains to life and godliness.

You must also believe that you're going to win – and you are going to win big.

Believe!

ANCHORED ACTIONS

Write out 10 believe sentences of affirmation that you believe. See the example below:

I believe I am God's masterpiece.

1. _____

2. _____

3. _____

4. _____

5. _____

6. _____

7. _____

8. _____

9. _____

10. _____

POINT TO PONDER

Do you believe that God is counting on you to make a change, to make a difference in your family?

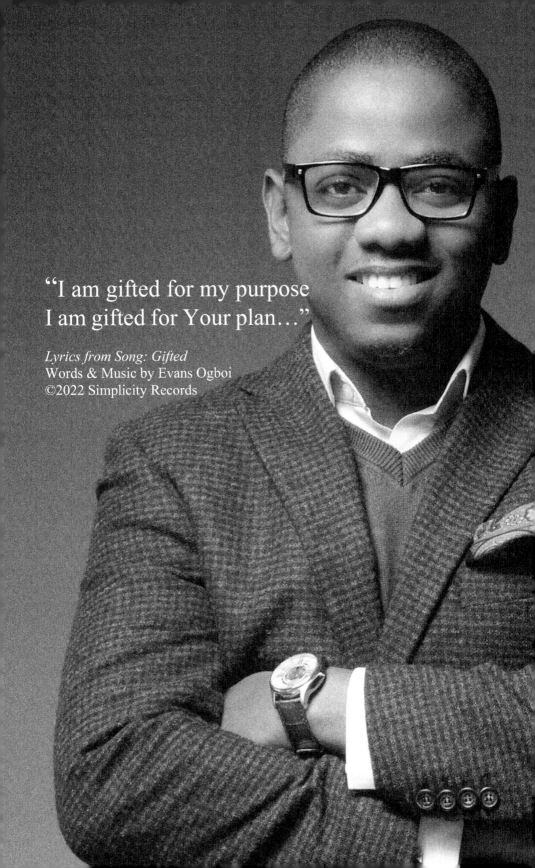

"I am gifted for my purpose
I am gifted for Your plan…"

Lyrics from Song: Gifted
Words & Music by Evans Ogboi
©2022 Simplicity Records

ANCHOR 2

PURPOSE

"The purpose of life is not to be happy. It is to be useful, to be honourable, to be compassionate, to have it make some difference that you have lived and lived well."

- Ralph Waldo Emerson

I HAVE SUPERPOWERS

*"For I know the plans I have for you, declares the LORD, plans to prosper you and not to harm you, plans to give you hope and a future." - **Jeremiah 29:11***

Super powers are an exceptional or extraordinary power or ability. At a certain point in your life, you will come to the realisation that you have been blessed with gifts, skills, or abilities that other people don't have.

That point of realization for me came when I was about thirteen years old. That is when I first discovered that I had *superpowers*.

I grew up in an age where there was a fascination for superheroes like Super Man, the hero with the cape that was faster than a speeding bullet, and Batman, who trolled the town of Gotham to rid it of its dangers.

But one superhero that always fascinated me was Peter Parker AKA Spider Man.

Let's backtrack a little bit. Parker started out a regular boy who unlocked extra ordinary powers after a spider's bite in a science laboratory. Sometimes I felt like Peter Parker, the way my love for music began. One minute I was like everyone else, and the next, everything changed.

In the year 1995, I lived with my parents and my siblings. I was a middle child, and like Peter Parker, there was nothing extraordinary about me.

"Evans, you're special," my mother would often say to me, before repeating the story of my birth. I had heard the story a thousand times before: After two miscarriages, lots of tears, prayers, and several prophecies, I was finally born - a beautiful, bouncing baby boy that had come to planet earth, ready to manifest.

I grew up listening to my mother's stories of my birth being special, but at the time, her words did not really mean much. I was quite sure a million kids had grown up hearing the same story.

My home was a regular Christian home with regular loving parents and regular loving siblings. I never really felt there was anything special about me.

When I turned thirteen, my *powers* unlocked in an unforgettable experience.

It was a late afternoon, I was in the living room of our three-bedroom flat in Benin City, Nigeria.

Like most teenagers my age, I was passionate about music, and I was constantly listening to a transistor radio that I carried around with me.

Suddenly, from the little radio playing music, I began to hear sounds, and they gave me access to dissect and separate sound from sound. I started to hear the different instruments, the distinct bass line, the plucking strings of the electric guitar, the drumbeat, the strings, the highs and lows of the piano – it was beautiful!

The different musical notes differentiated into various parts, and I could hear them distinctly – the harmony of the alto and tenor, and the distinct melody of the soprano voice.

It was like a scene from Spider Man where his senses were activated in the face of danger. It suddenly felt like the entire world was zooming in on me, and it felt like God opened my ears, announced a new dimension, and enabled me to access my innate gift of understanding music.

That is how my journey to *discovering* my purpose began.

God never created anyone empty.

Be determined to discover the treasure that lies inside of you and become dedicated to a life that seeks to mine your untapped potentials.

ANCHORED ACTIONS

1. What are some of the things that make you special? Write them down, no matter how insignificant you might think they are.

2. What thoughts have you had to deal with prior to this time that makes you think you do not have what it takes?

3. Read and meditate on Philippians 4:13.

   I can do all things through Christ that strengthens me!

POINTS TO PONDER

Be determined to discover the treasure that lies inside of you and become dedicated to a life that seeks to mine your untapped potentials.

FINDING *YOUR* SUPERPOWERS

*"Knowing your life purpose is the first step toward living a truly conscious life. A life of purpose provides us with a clear goal, a set finish line that you truly want to reach." - **Simon Foster***

Everyone has been born with something special, and that unique feature, gift, talent or ability defines your *purpose*. Purpose isn't really a destination, it's a process; it's a journey to understanding who you are and who you are becoming, as you apply yourself to what God has committed into your hands.

There is something God has given you; a gift God has graced you with. You might not know this, but everyone was born with a core purpose.

In acting we need to first understand what our assignment is. What is our core purpose? What has God created you to do on the face of the earth?

Finding purpose is one of the toughest things to do, and the search often leaves people wondering at certain points in their lives – what is my purpose? What is my assignment?

God has created you in His image and in His likeness, and has given you a purpose. The clues to your purpose are often found around you and have been built within you.

Birds have wings because they are built to fly.

Trees have roots because they are built to be in the ground.

Fishes have fins and gills because they are built to survive and thrive underwater.

What have you been built for?

Answering these questions accurately can point you to your purpose:

- *What problem have I been called to solve?*

- *What am I passionate about?*

- *What are my core gift and talents?*

Identifying your potential is key to anchoring success in life.

You need to understand what you've been created to do, and harness and work with the gifts God has put on the inside of you. You must hone your gift and ensure that it is ready to be used by God on the journey of life.

ANCHORED ACTIONS

Make a list of the skills, talents and gifts that you possess.

POINT TO PONDER

God has created you in His image and in His likeness and has given you a purpose. The things that can give you clues to your purpose are built within you.

NURTURING GIFTS

*"All the skilled and talented women spun thread with their hands, and brought what they had spun, blue and purple and scarlet fabric and fine linen." - **Exodus 35:25***

Have you ever had to care for a young plant? Or kept a pet? Or taken care of a baby? Whether it is a child, a pet, a plant, a dream or a talent, a level of tenderness is required to feed, groom and nourish it. That tenderness and care is called *nurturing*.

To nurture is to care for and protect (someone or something). Our talents and gifts, like babies need nurturing, and they need to be studied, understood, and enabled to develop.

In what ways do you nurture your talents and gifts?

What are your strengths and weaknesses? Which of your skills require practice? Who can you ask for help? How can you become better?

My teenager years progressed, and as I developed my gifts, I began to discover how specially God had created me. I loved the choir, and I had a passion for musical instruments; I loved to play the drums, the piano, and I loved to program music. I would take the keyboard home from church, where I worked overnight, programming, and recreating beats of popular songs.

At the time I did not know that God was using this phase of my life was a training ground to prepare me for what was ahead. I had no idea that all those hours I spent actively participating in the choir, learning to play the keyboard and the drums, was to sharpen my skills and gifts for my mission to the nations.

God was revealing to me, without me even knowing, that this was going to be the core of my future.

What do you have?

A gift?

A talent?

A skill?

Are you intentional about growing and grooming the gifts and graces that God has deposited in you?

It is important that after you discover and unlock your *superpowers* and find out what God has created you for, you deliberately begin to nurture your gifts.

It takes intense patience to improve your gifts. Be patient with yourself. Celebrate your small wins and continue to improve yourself.

ANCHORED ACTIONS

Spend some time to think of a plan to nurture your gifts, talents and skills. This could include getting more information online, taking up a new course, or spending time on practice. Your plan should include details of what you would spend your time doing, and how long you would nurture.

	Gift / Talent	Nurturing Plan
1.		
2.		
3.		
4.		
5.		

POINT TO PONDER

It is important that after you discover and unlock your *superpowers* and find out what God has created you for, you deliberately begin to nurture your gifts.

START WITH WHAT
YOU HAVE

"Though your beginning was small, yet your latter end would increase abundantly." - Job 8:7 NKJV

Often times, we are bogged down with thoughts such as: "I can't do it now, because I don't have..." or "I love doing this... but I'm not good enough, so I will wait till I'm good enough."

One of the most difficult things to do is *start*. If you always desire to start when everything is perfect, you *might* never find the right time, place, or be good enough to begin.

If you believe you were truly made to do this, then there is no better time than now; start with what you have!

In life there are no vacuums. God is an excellent creator, and nothing in this world was created empty. Everything has its place – the birds are naturally built to fly, the fish swim, and the trees are rooted to the ground. God created all creatures, with inbuilt capacity that is in line with their purpose.

It is the same way with me and you – in every one of us lies the innate capacity to fulfil our purpose.

THE PARABLE OF THE TALENTS

In the parable of the talents, Jesus tells the story of three individuals given talents by their master who proceeded to embark on a faraway journey.

The first individual was given five talents, the second, three talents, and the third individual was given one talent.

The individual that had five talents, went ahead to groom, and multiply his talent; the individual with two talents also multiplied his, but the person with the one talent did not do anything with it.

THE VALUE OF THE ONE

A lot of times we are like that man who had one talent.

We look at our one talent, and say to ourselves: *"I don't have much, what do I even have? I don't have anything – I have only one…"*

And with those words, we write ourselves off because we downplay the capacity and the enormous potential within us.

The bible also tells the story of two brothers – Esau and Jacob, and how Esau cheaply sold his birth-right to his brother for a bowl of soup!

Often, like Esau, we cast our *one* aside,

What is this birth-right to me?
What is this thing that I have?

A lot of times we talk down on what we have, disregard our *one talent*, and say we have nothing.

We cast our *one* aside, we sell it out, and every day we make decisions that trade our *one* for the momentarily satisfaction of a bowl of soup, and we end up not multiply our talent, or making productive use of it.

We complain and compare ourselves to the people that have five or three talents, and unknown to us, the one talent we have been blessed with has the potential to unlock massive impact on the earth!

Your one talent might be the key to liberation: and a much-needed solution to the world's puzzling problems.

There is greatness within you, and your one talent is potential within you.

You've got to believe *'I've got something'*.

What is that in your hand?

The Lord asked Moses that question when he was sending him out on a mission.

This was not just any ordinary mission; it was one that Moses had been born and prepared for. The potential to deliver the Israelites from captivity had been in him for many years, and even though he had run away and hidden in a dessert land, working as a shepherd, on a certain day, the Lord came looking for him. In a life changing encounter, the Lord asked Moses:

"What is that in your hand?"

In Moses' hand, he held a shepherd's staff, but he had dismissed it, and ignorantly thought it was *just a staff* that he had used to herd his flock of sheep. Unknown to him, the staff, just like Moses, was a mighty measure of potential.

The story of Moses and his staff is similar to the story of the widow and Elijah.

There was famine in the land, and the Lord had sent Elijah to a widow who was to provide sustenance for him. Elijah showed up at her doorstep and asked her: "What do you have in your house?"

All she had was a little oil. And that was all he needed for a miracle to burst forth.

You have something!

What do you have?

A dream?

A talent?

A vision?

An idea?

There's always something, you've got what it takes! Don't neglect it, push it under the carpet, or compare it to anyone else's.

Start with what you have!

The bible admonishes us do not despise the days of small beginnings.

You must realise that though your beginning may be small, your latter end will be great.

You must run with this in mind.

Jesus, for the joy that was set before him humbled himself to the death of the cross.

Start, not only to satisfy the fact that you've started.

Start with the end in mind knowing that I'm going to win

Start!

ANCHORED ACTIONS

Go back to the plan you created in the previous chapter. Adjust the plan and highlight the things you can begin right away, with the resources, and what is available to you NOW

POINT TO PONDER

God is such an excellent creator, that he never created anything empty. In every one of us lies the innate capacity to fulfil our purpose.

"More of You is my desire,
I'm desperate for You.
Speak Lord, and I'll obey…"

Lyrics from Song: Take me Back
Words & Music by Evans Ogboi
©2022 Simplicity Records

ANCHOR 3

COMMISSIONED

"The more we tarry in God's presence, the more we become like Him daily, which ultimately puts us at the centre of His will."

- Evans Ogboi

FINDING GOD

*"I cry out to God Most High, to God who fulfils his purpose for me." - **Psalm 57:2***

Finding God is an intentional process of seeking and initiating a deeper relationship with Him. We all need a deeper commitment with our Creator to fulfil our destiny to its fullest.

Daniel 11:32b says: *"They that do know their God shall do exploits."* In other words, you must know Him; His ways, patterns, and principles to fulfil your mandate on earth.

Discovering the gifts and talents that stand you out from a jostling crowd is one thing, connecting with God and discovering the reason *why* He has given you these gifts in the first place is another.

You are on a mission, and all the gifts you manifest are divinely orchestrated by God and have been given to you to meet a specific need.

Finding God is the first step to unlocking the *reason* God has created you. You can unlock your purpose, but if you do not know *why* God has called you, you might never *fulfil* the purpose God has given you.

In the late nineties, I was enthusiastic about playing music, but I did not have a real relationship with God, but the year 2000 changed everything for me; it was the year I found God.

In the last few days leading to 1999, there was a buzz about the world ending once the clock struck twelve, and the world moved into the millennium.

I was terrified of the world ending, and like many other young people, I thought the world as we knew it would cease to exist. Therefore, I attended the crossover service with trepidation, repenting of all my sins, and preparing earnestly to meet my maker.

After the clock struck twelve, and we crossed into the very dreaded year 2000, I waited, but it never showed up.

There were no explosions.

No end of the world events or rumblings.

Nothing happened.

Except the shout of jubilations that erupted from the excited worshippers that filled the church.

"Happy New Year!"

I almost had a heart attack. I thought the world had ended, and in that moment, I realised that even though I led worship in church, and played the keyboard, I did not have a relationship with God.

After service that morning, on the first day of 2000, I got home and got on my knees and said a sincere prayer:

"Lord, I want to be serious with you. I do not want to live in fear. God if you would help me on this journey, I will follow you and serve you all my life."

That was the day I made a dedication and a personal decision to make Jesus the Lord of my life. God has been faithful to that prayer till date. I found God, and that is when my journey to fulfilling my purpose began.

ANCHORED ACTIONS

Do you have a relationship with God?

If you do not have a relationship with God and would like to, please say this prayer:

> *Lord Jesus, I ask that you come into my life, and you fix me and make me whole. I desire to have a relationship with you. Cleanse me of all the things I have done wrong in the past. Have your way in my life.*

POINT TO PONDER

I found God, and that is when my journey to fulfilling my purpose began.

Understanding the uniqueness of your assignment is key to the fulfilment of your purpose.

CREATING UNENDING VALUE

*"Don't forget to do good and to share what you have because God is pleased with these kinds of sacrifices." - **Hebrews 13:16***

In the words of Dr. Myles Monroe, "your value in life is determined by the problems you solve through your gifts… if you want to become successful seek to become a person of value."

Value refers to the relative worth, utility, importance or significance of an individual. The extent of your *usefulness* determines the extent of your growth and expansion. It is expected that we create unending value and bless humanity with the gifts God has bestowed upon us. The day you stop creating value, you become irrelevant to your world.

Understanding the uniqueness of your assignment is key to the fulfilment of your purpose. Purpose is entrenched in service and creating value, and it is hinged on using your gifts to solve a problem.

The minute I found God, and had understood my purpose, I began to serve with my gift, volunteering with churches that were starting out and needed help with leading worship.

I served in several groups, and not long afterwards, I began to travel to various cities in Nigeria. I was attending gospel concerts, and ministering in song, sometimes alongside my friend, Elvis Ediagbonya who is currently an established music professional in the Netherlands.

I grew with a service culture, and a desire to use my gift to be a blessing.

After I moved from Benin City to Lagos, I joined RCCG Straight Gate Parish at Faramobi Ajike in Lagos, Nigeria. During the time I was there, I served in the Teens Church department, specifically the teenage choir, and the music department.

From there, I moved to Fountain of Life Victoria Island Parish under the pastorate of Pastor Olumide Olugbenle to continue in service. I also served in the Teens ministry, and would gather the young people together occasionally, to teach them the Scriptures. I was very committed to the choir, where I served as a drummer, sometimes as a keyboardist and a lot of times, teaching the choir new songs. For a few years, I continued to serve in these areas.

I travelled across northern Nigeria, with a missionary group for a few weeks, and was in the worship team and charged with leading the choir, playing the keyboard, programming music, and directing music for crusades.

Shortly afterwards, we started traveling to neighbouring countries like Ghana, and other parts as I continued to grow in service. I was committed to helping other people with their music ministries, and my journey as a music producer started with me helping other music ministers make music and programming the keyboard to create accompanying tracks for their songs.

I continued doing this for a long time, and unknown to me, this was God's way of leading into one of the areas I would work largely – music production.

In creating value, you become passionate about solving problems; you become obsessed with solutions and your life becomes an answer to questions, prayers; and a person of unending value.

Creating value makes you a happier person, and when you show up on the scene, everyone around you becomes happy because you are an answer.

ANCHORED ACTIONS

1. Make a list of areas where your gift and talents are needed. Create a plan on how to use them in those areas.

2. Make a list of the problems you are passionate about solving.

3. Identify the group of people you believe you have been called to serve.

POINTS TO PONDER

In creating value, you become passionate about solving problems; you become obsessed with solutions and your life becomes an answer to questions, prayers; and a person of unending value.

THE SECRET PLACE

"Whether you turn to the right or to the left, your ears will hear a voice behind you, saying, 'This is the way; walk in it." - *ISIAH 30:21*

The Secret Place is not just any place, it is the place of prayer that brings us under the covering of God. Psalms 91: 1 says: *"He that dwells in the secret place of the Most High shall abide under the shadow of the Almighty"*

How often do you dwell in the Secret Place? Do you dwell and abide, or do you pay occasional visits to the Secret Place? The more we tarry in God's presence, the more we become like Him daily, which ultimately puts us at the centre of His will.

Faramobi Ajike

That is the name of the street in Anthony Village, Lagos where I lived with my friend Elvis. At the time, I was a teenager, and miles away from my parents in Benin City. From that location, God began to call me into a deeper place of concentration.

At the time, all Elvis and I wanted to do was make music; we were young, talented and had no responsibilities or cares in the world.

Although I was a Christian, and devoted to living upright and serving God, I was at a place where I could have gotten distracted by the thrills and frills that life had to offer.

There was a church that stood along Faramobi Ajike Street; it was a stone's throw from where I lived. With the exceptions of Sunday mornings, and some weekday evenings, nothing much happened there; and it usually stood quiet, but with each passing day, there was a growing desire to go to the empty church and pray.

I followed the prompt. The Lord led me to a secret place of prayer; everyday met me there in that church praying fervently, and consistently, and studying the word of God. My understanding of the things of God increased, and the wisdom of God grew in me. This was how my relationship with God developed, especially as I began to hear the voice of the Spirit. I grew immensely – I was receiving directions on what to do and what steps to take.

It was in those moments that I was led to go to the bookshop of the church where I worshipped, *Fountain of Life*, Victoria Island parish, to purchase a book. The book was titled: *In Pursuit of Purpose* by Dr. Myles Munroe.

I read that book and my entire perspective changed. After reading the book, I had a strong impression in my Spirit that God had taken me on a journey and brought me to this point to make a decision that would change the trajectory of my life.

I was led to embark on a three-day fasting and prayer retreat, to seek the Lord's voice, and direction regarding my course of study, and what I would spend the rest of my life doing.

After the retreat, I found clarity. I knew for certain that God was leading me to serve in the music ministry, full time. I did not have everything I required for this to happen, but I knew the direction I was to focus on.

There and then, I decided to serve in the music ministry full time, this meant I would study music, and focus on it completely.

However, I had to discuss this with my parents; and the thought brought some measure of concern.

My mom had always been my number one cheerleader and fan, but my dad had other plans. He had always wanted me to study Accounting, and I was concerned about how he would receive the news that I was to study music.

I summoned courage and with the help of the Holy Spirit, I had a lengthy conversation with my dad.

He listened intently to me and at the end of our discussion, he looked at me and said: "*Yes, do it, study music professionally, and do it in London.*"

God be praised!

This was confirmation of my prayers, many of which I had prayed in my secret place, where God had given me a blueprint and had also showed me the exact steps I needed to take to execute it.

ANCHORED ACTIONS

Create a secret place of prayer where you can hone your relationship with God.

Listen and obey the Holy Spirit.

POINT TO PONDER

The more we tarry in God's presence, the more we become like Him daily, which ultimately puts us at the centre of His will.

"You've been working real hard with tears in your eyes… And it seems you're about to give up now Cos it seems all hope is lost. Try Christ, my child, He hears your cry…"

Lyrics from Song: Taste and See
Words & Music by Evans Ogboi

ANCHOR 4

PROCESS

"Between you and the manifestation of your dream is *time*, and within that time window, exists a process and a journey, which you must master."

- Evans Ogboi

CONSISTENCY

*"And let us not grow weary of doing good, for in due season we will reap, if we do not give up." - **Galatians 6:9***

Consistency is the habit of greatness. Firmness is the virtue you need to withstand the opposition that seeks to stop you. How firm are you about your decision to reach the top?

Accomplishing greatness is often preceded by *focus*. The road to success is paved with uncertainty, doubts and struggles; to succeed, you must develop the ability to narrow in and focus, irrespective of what is happening around you.

Consistency is the art of remaining on track, and on the same course, even with the passage of time. You must be determined to succeed. The process is usually tedious, but only the brave pull through, only the persistent and only the strong make it to the finish line.

There is a biblical story of Joseph, a young lad who had a massive dream. Between Joseph's dream and its manifestation was one crucial factor – time.

Between you and the manifestation of your dream is time, and within that time, there is a process, and a journey, which you must master. You can achieve this by being consistent.

How many *Nos* are you ready to take? How many times are you willing to try and fail?

I know a doctor who wrote a professional exam seven times and only passed at the seventh attempt. To say this in simpler terms, he failed the same examination six times!

I knew first-hand how tough and how challenging it was for his family, and how heart-breaking it was for every time he had to retake the same exam, but on the seventh time, there was success!

The road to success requires strength and determination with focus to remain consistent until the desired result is achieved.

Success is only for those who are willing to persevere, stay, go through the storm, stand the test of time and emerge victorious. Everyone has the capacity, but success is really a choice. You will win if you choose not to quit!

ANCHORED ACTIONS

Write out a list of things you would like to be consistent at, and practice being consistent about the things you have written on the list.

- Do it for 7 days

- Do it for 2 weeks

- Do it for 1 month

- Do it for 3 months

POINT TO PONDER

Between you and the manifestation of your dream is *time*, and within that time window, exists a process and a journey, which you must master.

MULTIPLY

*"Let every skilful craftsman among you come and make all that the LORD has commanded." - **Exodus 35:10***

Multiplying connotes great increase. You must develop yourself to remain relevant to your world.

Soon after I decided to major in the music ministry, I developed a hunger for personal development. I began studying and taking trainings and courses.

One of my dreams was to travel abroad and study music professionally, and I began applying to schools abroad. Specifically, I remember a school, *Berklee College of Music* in Boston.

I applied for a scholarship, and I put everything into it. I filled out the application, created the recordings I was required to include in my application, and I sent it in. I prayed, believed God, and I was waiting expectantly.

When I got word from *Berklee*, I was in shock. They had declined my application.

I was heartbroken. I felt like everything was over, it felt like this *was the end of it*. It took a lot to get myself together and I asked, 'Lord, what next?'

However, this opened a new chapter in my life.

At the time, I had a meeting with a blessed gentleman at my church, Mr. Peter Longe, an incredible support and a destiny helper. I can never forget his encouraging words and what he said to me:

"Evans, Boston and *Berkley College of Music* may not have come through, but what else can you do with the time that you have? What else can you find locally to do in Africa?"

The conversation with Mr. Peter Longe opened my mind for the first time to a new chapter, and the possibilities that existed where I was. I realised I had a potential to start something small, and then multiply my efforts.

He asked me to look for the best school in West Africa and after my research and discovered that the Lagos State government had set up Eko Reel Mix studios, one of the most equipped at the time, and had also had a training programme.

The studio was in the same state I was located and was easily accessible. I did not need a visa to get there – this was something I could do right away. I also got my first sponsorship and support, as Mr. Peter Longe paid half my tuition and training costs. I enrolled for the programme at Eko Reel Mix Studio, and successfully completed that course.

It was at Eko Reel Mix that I recorded my debut album, *Miracle* in 2007. It was also at Eko Reel Mix that I started to produce full time and from there not long after, I set up my own studio and I registered my music business, *Simplicity Records.*

Multiplicity is guaranteed as you create unending value as you remain consistent.

As you remain doggedly focused on what you have been called to do, irrespective of challenges, you shall multiply!

ANCHORED ACTIONS

1. What are the things you can do to upscale your talent or gift?

2. What medium can you exploit to expand your talent or gift?

POINT TO PONDER

As you remain doggedly focused on what you have been called to do, irrespective of your challenges, you shall multiply!

SUPERNATURAL SUPPLY

"All things work together for the good of them, that love the Lord, to them that are called according to His purpose." - **RomanS 8:28**

Supernatural supply is an abundance from heaven that we experience when God comes through for His children.

We serve a living God who can meet all our needs according to His riches, not according to our human economic power.

Several years prior, I was in a team leading worship at a church event. The Ministering Pastor was visiting from America, and as the worship progressed, he turned to the team and addressed us directly, and openly.

"One of you in this group is embarking on higher educational learning abroad. The Lord said to tell that person that: ***He's going to send supernatural supply..***"

At the time, I did not think much of what the Pastor had said, especially as all my pursuits to study internationally had met with roadblocks, and I was currently enrolled in a course at Eko Reel Mix.

After my course, doors opened for me, and things started happening quickly. I recorded my debut album, I was working as a producer, traveling widely to spread the gospel by ministering at church events, and I was using the best of my gift to the glory of God. I was living out my purpose, but inwardly, I knew there was a *next level*.

By the inspiration of the Spirit, I decided to seek admission to a music school one more time. I remember walking along the street, and I heard the Lord clearly whisper to me: 'What about SAE?'

SAE was one of the schools I had admired for years. It is a global institute for sound engineering and music production and the creative arts. They had opened a campus in London.

By the leading of the Spirit, I went to the cybercafé where I sent a direct email to SAE, requesting if they had acquired the license which would enable them to admit international students. I received an affirmative response shortly afterwards.

Consequently, I sent in an application to SAE. My application submission included my transcript and the work I had previously recorded at *Eko Reel Mix Studio*. I remained optimistic, while I waited to get a response from the school. A few weeks later, I received the email saying I had been accepted and that I had to start the registration process by paying a fee.

THIS WAS GREAT NEWS!

In an interesting twist of events, all the things I had done within my waiting period had qualified me for my application at *SAE*.

I needed to raise the money for my tuition fee and visa appointment fees which was on the high side as it was beyond what I could afford. As I thought about the fees I required to travel to the UK, I suddenly remembered the word the visiting Pastor had spoken several months prior.

God will send supernatural supply!

I held on to that word and every time I prayed about my studies in the UK, I always prayed for supernatural supply. I chose not to worry, and instead, I trusted the Lord. God came through for me and made a way where there was no way. God sent supernatural supplies, and my tuition and visa fees were paid!

Heaven is committed to a life that is committed to God's purpose. You will never lack supply for your journey.

In times of need, remember you have a Heavenly Father who can make provision, all you need to do is call on God's Headquarters, and provision for the vision would be made available by Him.

God is faithful!

ANCHORED ACTIONS

In what areas of your life do you require supernatural supply? List them out and trust God to make provision for you.

POINT TO PONDER

Heaven is committed to a life that is committed to God's purpose. You will never lack supply for your journey.

THINK POSITIVE

*"They will have no fear of bad news; their hearts are steadfast, trusting in the Lord." - **Psalm 112:7 (kjv)***

As a man thinketh in his heart so is he. Your thoughts determine your output in life. The right thoughts will ultimately put you in the right place and conversely, negative thoughts will put you in a ditch.

Thinking positive is such a game changer! Everything about your life starts to change for good when you start to think positive.

Thinking positive sometimes is a struggle, especially if you have dealt with negative situations for a long time. Sometimes it is hard to break free from a cycle of negativity.

I had been granted admission to SAE, one of the top music schools in London, and had miraculously paid my tuition fees. All that stood between me and my dreams was a visa to the United Kingdom.

As I filled out the student visa application, one thought was heavy on my heart. In the past, I had applied four times for a visiting visa to the United Kingdom, and all four times, the UK Home Office had denied my requests. What if that happened again?

Getting this visa was my last resort. Asides from the fact that I had spent everything I had, the person I was putting up with had just kicked me out, and I suddenly had nowhere to live.

I called another friend to ask if I could stay with him, and he declined. I called another friend, who had also declined but I knew there was no other option, so I had to head there even when he declined and I said you know what, *'you're going to have to push me out yourself!'*

I managed to buy some time with my friend, and he agreed I could stay with him for a few weeks, just enough time to get my visa and travel to the United Kingdom. My agreement with him was after that time had elapsed, I would have to leave.

I was walking on the thin line of faith – marking time and praying my visa application would be successful, and everything would go as I had planned. Otherwise, I would have no other choice but to return to Benin City.

I got the news shortly that my passport was ready for collection, but I also realised that the greatest battle I had to fight was the one within.

As I headed to the Visa Application Centre, the negative voices kept pounding in my head:

You're a failure
This is a mistake; this is not going to work out.
This is just another major disappointment waiting to happen.
You're about to be thrown into another huge pit of despair.

Getting this visa was my last resort, my last chance to make it work, everything was centred on it, and as I inched closer to the visa collection centre, the enemy kept piling negative words in my head.

It is not going to work...
It is not going to happen...
You are finished...

It was so bad, I almost fell off the commercial bike I was on, and I was losing strength and willpower. Just as these thoughts were bombarding my head and my heart, another voice came from deep within.

What if everything falls perfectly into place?
What if you have been granted a visa?

Those words were a ray of light in a darkened world, and I was strengthened by that positive thought.

What if I have been granted a visa?

It suddenly seemed like there was a war within me as the positive and negative thoughts battled to take root in my heart.

The negative thoughts were trolling my head.

You're a failure. This is the end. This is it for you.'

The positive thoughts were reaffirming, revalidating and reassuring:

What if I am a granted a visa! This would be the beginning for me, and the launch of a greater beginning!

I got to the visa application centre and picked up the large envelope where my passport was enclosed. Even though I had been instructed not to open the package, as I walked down the stairs and towards the exit, I ripped the envelope open, and began to flip through my passport, with trepidation in my heart.

I flipped the first time, and I did not see anything, then I flipped the second time and the third time, and I saw a glint, something that looked like a visa.

My heart skipped for joy.

I opened the passport, and right smack on one of its pages was my visa. After four refusals, I had finally been issued a student visa to study in the United Kingdom!

It was a dream come true.

Friends, is there a possibility that you receive all the things you are trusting God for?

I want to challenge your curiosity.

I want to challenge your mindset.

I want to provoke you to begin to think positive thoughts concerning your circumstance and your situation.

Yes, it is possible that you will live in super health for the rest of your life!

Yes, it is possible that your family can be together again!

Yes, it is possible that you can build a business or career and excel at it!

Yes, it is possible that you can reach your goal!

I challenge you to think positive thoughts concerning your life and your destiny.

Remember that everything starts with how you think. The Bible says, *As a man thinketh in his heart, so is he.*

So, think positive thoughts!

I am favoured!

I am blessed!

I will achieve my dreams!

I will succeed!

It will happen for me!

Remain positive and enjoy a life of limitless possibilities.

ANCHORED ACTIONS

Write out ten positive declarations and read them aloud.

POINTS TO PONDER

Thinking positive is such a game changer! Everything about your life starts to change for good when you start to think positive.

FIGHT!

*"Rise up; this matter is in your hands. We will support you, so take courage and do it." - **Ezra 10:4 (NIV)***

To fight means to struggle to overcome and eliminate what stands on your path to greatness. Fight the good fight of faith – only the violent take it by force.

God has given you what you need to fulfil destiny, but you must press through to lay hold of it. At the entrance to every land flowing with milk and honey, there are giants to overpower. Every child of God, like the Israelites must fight to possess the land.

A while ago, God showed me a vision, and two stories in the bible that matched, one in the New Testament and the other in the Old Testament.

In the Old Testament, during the period of Moses' birth, a decree was pronounced that every firstborn was to be killed.

God gave me a revelation in the realm of the spirit – in the season where Moses was to be born, there was a trigger. Something was about to happen that would cause a huge shift, and in the realm of the spirit, demons were released to stop that word from happening. On Earth, a decree was passed by Pharaoh, and every male born child was to be killed. All male children birthed in that season were murdered because there was an attack on the destiny of Moses.

God led the mother of Moses to leave her baby in a basket for the Egyptian princess to find, and because of his mother's act of faith, Moses' life was spared. Moses was placed in the court of the man who was seeking to kill him, and he was raised by that same man.

Isn't God, amazing?

The second story in the New Testament is that of the birth of Jesus. In the same season that Jesus was to be born, it was picked up in the realm of the Spirit.

The wise men had seen His birth in the stars, and they had gone to the king to tell him that something was about to happen, and a king was to be born.

The reigning king was troubled by their news, and at the same period, a decree was made that every male baby should be killed.

By the wisdom of God, and the leading of the Spirit, baby Jesus was taken away by his parents to the safety of Egypt.

The same series of events happened in two different dispensations. In both scenarios, a decree was passed that every baby boy was to be killed, and it was all about the kingdom of darkness trying to war against the kingdom of God.

Your life is no different, and the minute you were conceived in your mother's womb, there was a trigger.

In the realm of the spirit, an announcement heralded your birth, and you may not know it, but many of the battles you have fought all your life have not just been about you, but your destiny!

The devil could not succeed in taking you out before you came to earth, but the minute you landed on planet earth, it became a battle between the kingdom of darkness and the kingdom of God.

In the book of Ephesians, 6 :12, it says:

We wrestle not against flesh and blood, but against principalities, against spiritual wickedness in heavenly places, against the rulers of darkness in this age.

Therefore, you must realise that we are not fighting against flesh and blood or people we can see, but we are battling invisible spirits, and the principalities and powers who are working night and day to stop you.

How are you going to win this war? How are you going to overcome and come out the other side, a winner, and a victor?

You need the help of the Holy Spirit.

Your destiny is real.

The adversary is real.

Your helper is real, which is Jesus and his Spirit living in you.

Your destiny is worth your fight. Remember you're not fighting alone; you're fighting with the help of the Spirit.

Fight the good fight of faith.

ANCHORED ACTIONS

- Have you been told how great your destiny is?

- Do you believe your destiny is great?

- List the different things you can do to protect and advance your destiny?

POINTS TO PONDER

God has given you what you need to fulfil destiny, but you must press through to lay hold of it. At the entrance to every land flowing with milk and honey, there are giants to overpower. Every child of God, like the Israelites must fight to possess the land.

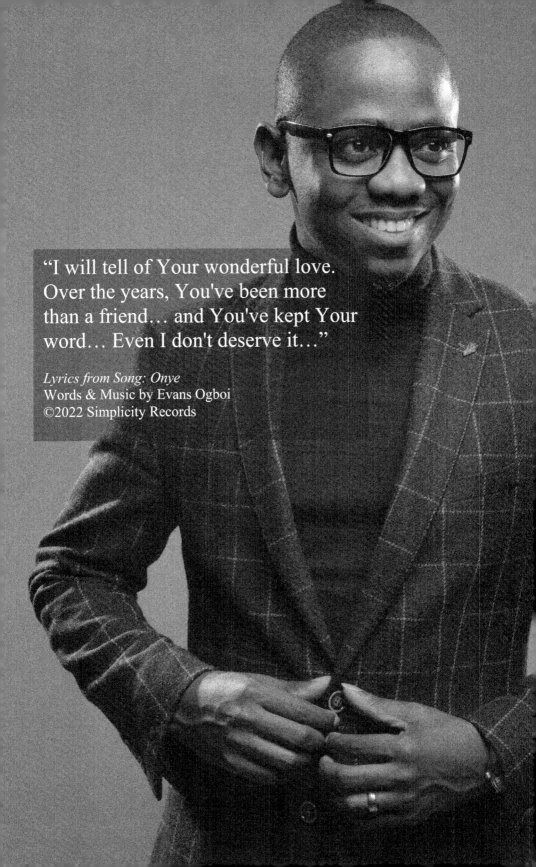

"I will tell of Your wonderful love. Over the years, You've been more than a friend… and You've kept Your word… Even I don't deserve it…"

Lyrics from Song: Onye
Words & Music by Evans Ogboi
©2022 Simplicity Records

ANCHOR 5

RELATIONSHIPS

"We all need help and support, and as we journey through life, we must bear in mind that our blessings come from God *through men*."

- Evans Ogboi

HELPERS OF DESTINY

"Because I rescued the poor who cried for help, and the fatherless who had none to assist them. The one who was dying blessed me; I made the widow's heart sing." - Job 29:12-13

Divine helpers are people sent by God to grant you ease and possibilities in the fulfilment of destiny. We all need help and support, and as we journey through life, we must bear in mind that our blessings come from God *through men.*

Jesus built noteworthy relationships, and by the leading of the Spirit, Jesus handpicked His disciples, and they turned out to be the right people called to work with Him, for the redemption of mankind.

These people were charged with the responsibility of taking the work Jesus had begun to the next level, and they formed the bedrock of the church that spread all over the world.

The same is true with us!

We need people, and we cannot overemphasise the gift of men, however, it is important that by the help of the Holy Spirit, we are led to the *right people.*

There have been stories where the wrong people with the wrong influences, destroyed destinies. The Bible puts it this way in Ephesians 15:33 –

"Evil communication corrupts good manners."

As you seek to build healthy relationships and walk into relationships that will take you to the next level in your destiny, it is important to pray ceaselessly about the people that God would send your way.

I call them helpers of DESTINY.

The beauty of life is that we are blessed to be a blessing.

The scriptures say in Genesis 8:22: *"as long as the earth remains, seedtime and harvest shall not cease."*

As we receive help, we invariably become helpers of others destiny; and the world becomes a better place when we help each other walk into our manifestation of destiny.

ANCHORED ACTIONS

1. Look at your current circle. Make a list of the people who have helped you in your journey. Make another list of people you have helped in their journey.

2. If you do not have the right people in your life, commit to asking God to send you destiny helpers as you walk with Him daily.

3. List out areas in which you need destiny helpers and map out a pattern to pray concerning it.

POINT TO PONDER

Divine helpers are people sent by God to grant you ease and possibilities in the fulfilment of destiny. We all need help and support, and as we journey through life, we must bear in mind that our blessings come from God *through men*.

THE PRAYER KEY

"Don't worry about anything. Instead, pray about everything. Tell God what you need and thank him for all he has done." - **PHILIPIANS 4:6**

We need people to work with, to achieve our God-given purpose. Of the 7.3 billion people on the surface of the earth, *where* and *how* do we locate the people God has sent to us? Prayer works wonders!

Often people argue that God is a Supreme Being, and already knows what we need before we even ask. The question often arises: *Do we need to pray?*

The Holy Spirit taught me early in my life journey to ask God and pray about *everything!*

Although God knows what we desire, the Bible encourages us in Matthew 7 verse 7 to ask:

"Ask, and it shall be given unto you seek and you shall find knock and the door shall be opened unto you."

Prayer is a blank cheque given to us to communicate with the Creator regarding everything.

I knew I could not achieve what was before me all by myself, and I did not know how to find the people with the right combination that would help me unlock the potential within me. Every day I prayed consistently and asked God to lead me to meet the right people – my destiny helpers, and specifically, my life partner.

I was not sure where they were on the face of the earth, but I consistently prayed, and asked the Lord to orchestrate our feet and cause our paths to cross. It was not long after these series of prayers that I met my lovely wife, Purist, and several other people who are highly significant in my life and is instrumental to my success.

It is incredible how God answers prayers.

Irish poet, Joseph Medlicott Scriven's wrote the words of *What a Friend we have in Jesus*, a song that went on to become one of the most popular Christian songs of all times. One of my favourite stanzas reads thus:

> *"Oh, what needless pain we bear, all because we do not carry everything to God in prayer."*

Jesus answers prayers and my life is a testimony of the fact.

Determine to carry *everything* to God in prayer. No matter what your desires are, you must believe that as you pray, the answers are sure to manifest!

ANCHORED ACTIONS

1. Have you ever prayed about having the right spouse, leaders, neighbours, colleagues, and friends?

2. Write down prayers about connecting with people according to God's will for your life. It is not too early to pray about it today.

POINT TO PONDER

Every day I prayed consistently and asked God to lead me to meet the right people – my destiny helpers, and specifically, my life partner.

MASTER PLANNER

"I planted the seed, Apollos watered it, but God made it grow. So, neither he who plants nor he who waters is anything, but only God, who makes things grow. The man who plants and the man who waters have one purpose, and each will be rewarded according to his own labour." - **1corinthians 3:6-9**

God is a master planner. When He connects you with your divine helpers, He orchestrates events and connects the dots to your favour; He has everything in His plans and does not leave a single detail out. Trust Him!

In 2010, Purist and I were in a four-year committed relationship, and working towards getting married.

Unexpectedly, during her final year in the University of Benin, she decided to withdraw from her course to follow her passion in music. Fortunately, she miraculously gained admission to a Music school in the UK and with the support of her father, she travelled to begin her studies in Music.

Purist's departure was an episode of joy for us, although I had not met with her father to make my intentions known due to his decision to ensure Purist finished college before planning for marriage.

However, I was hopeful and often reminded God in prayers about how I needed a replication of the same miracle, and subsequently I began my application to SAE.

In January 2011, I landed at Heathrow Airport, in the United Kingdom!

Months earlier, I remember that I had a dream where I saw myself sitting on a platform, where I could see houses, and I suddenly began to move in an opposite direction to the houses. I remember that I had awakened from my dream, confused, as I did not understand it.

Could this be the spirit of backwardness? I had wondered to myself at the time.

On the day I landed in the United Kingdom, and sat on the train heading to my school, I looked out through the side window, and behold, I was moving in one direction, and the houses were moving in the opposite direction. This was exactly what I had been seen in my dream!

My dream had simply been of me sitting in a train in London, on this very day!

Months ago, who would have known that this would happen, except God, the Master Planner, who had positioned people in my life to provide support, motivation, and resources to get me where I was?

Within a few months of being in the UK, God was faithful to introduce me to a man that would be a father to me. This man was my pastor, Pastor Chris Adeoye. I also met his lovely wife, Pastor Abi Adeoye. They were the pastors of RCCG church, Living Faith Connections, where I gained employment to work as a Music Minister and Choir Director.

The Lord had orchestrated my steps. I had prayed for my divine helpers and the Lord had directed my steps to meet the right people, and work in an environment where I was loved, cherished, and nurtured to become who God had called me to be.

Eventually, I ended up meeting Purist's father, and things moved very quickly. Within a space of six months of meeting her father in Nigeria, Purist and I were married, and Pastor Chris Adeoye flew down to Nigeria to perform the ceremony.

All the things that had seemed impossible mountains before me, by the grace of God, had been levelled to the ground. God had ensured that everything worked together for my good, and everything had fallen into place. When I think of it all now, God was at the master controls, planning the entire thing.

Sometimes when we meet our divine helpers, we want to *work it out* ourselves, but God is the master planner, and has a perfect plan waiting for us. God knows exactly what He has created for you; the pathway to your destiny – He has laid it all out.

It is important that we trust in Him completely with our hearts and the affairs of our lives. The scripture Proverbs 3:5 puts it this way:

"Trust in the Lord with all your heart and lean not on your own understanding, in all your ways acknowledge Him and He shall direct your path."

ANCHORED ACTIONS

1. Can you make a list of the times in your life when God came through for you?

2. What current journeys are you embarking on, and are you trusting Him to complete?

POINTS TO PONDER

God knows exactly what He has created for you; the pathway to your destiny – He has laid it all out.

It is important that we trust in Him completely with our hearts and the affairs of our lives.

"…When you're down and lonely and you don't know what to do… Lift your hands to the sky and know He'll be right there…"

Lyrics from Song: Taste and See
Words & Music by Evans Ogboi
©2022 Simplicity Records

ANCHOR 6

ADVERSITY

———— 66 ————

"When the troubles of life knock at your door, do not be dismayed; look up to Jesus!"

- Evans Ogboi

———— 99 ————

CURVEBALL

"When the enemy shall come in like a flood, the Spirit of the LORD shall lift up a standard against him." - **Psalm 59:19b**

Acurveball is an unexpected turn of events initiated by an opponent or chance. In life, we will surely face adversity, as life throws so many unexpected twists and turns. No journey is easy, and no path is smooth all through.

Even the Bible tells us:

> *In the world ye shall have tribulation: but be of good cheer; I have overcome the world. -* ***John.16.33***

What do you do when everything is working so well for you and suddenly, something happens that throws you off balance?

There are times when life comes at you like a flood, and an unexpected event occurs that challenges everything that you have ever known about God.

You might have a growing relationship with God, where everything you ask for *comes to pass*, and then a massive challenge comes that you cannot understand or explain; a challenge that might shake you to your very foundation, and make you question even your own stance in God. Challenges can happen to even the good people in life. No one is exempt.

It happened to me in 2007.

I was excited about my newfound passion and career path; I had written and produced songs, and was ready to release my debut album, titled *Miracle*.

I put together a choir – mostly made up of my musician-friends, and we had been practicing and rehearsing hard, working towards a live recording and official launch of the album.

I got the news that my dad had an accident and had gone into a coma. Instantly, my heart was divided. I was closely in touch with my family in Benin, praying and trying to remain quiet in my spirit, and focused on the assignment and what God had me do with my project.

Three days after the accident, I was at a night rehearsal when I received a phone call from my sister that changed everything.

I could hear her crying at the other end, but I could not make out what she was saying. With a beating heart, I walked away from the noisy environment, and I heard her words in a haze. "Daddy has stopped breathing."

My world froze.

Everything stopped.

I never thought this would ever happen. I had been praying for my parents decreeing that they would live long to see their children's children.

'How could God do this to me?' I thought, 'how could this happen? Dad was meant to recover and get back on his feet. The Holy Spirit did not tell me this would happen!'

As I was thinking these thoughts, I suddenly received the peace of God at my heart. The first thing I did was take the cordless microphone and walk out of our rehearsal space, away from the rest of the team, and into the surrounding fields. I lifted my eyes to the heavens and began to sing:

Praise God from whom all blessings flow.
Praise Him all creatures here below.
Praise Him above ye heavenly host. Praise Father, Son, and Holy Ghost.

The rest of the team did not understand what was happening at the time, but they heard me sing, and they were just flowing with the music as they would usually do, they joined me to sing, and we worshiped the Lord.

I lifted my eyes to the heavens and continued to worship God. There was a battle going on inside my head, my heart was beating fast, but I kept singing to Jesus, and worshiping the Father.

The Lord ministered strength to my heart, and after that session of rehearsal, we ended the meeting.

Early the next day, I travelled to Benin City, and on getting home, the reality dawned. Dad was really gone.

What was going to become of our family? How would we survive? How had this happened in the first place? Was this an attack? What had gone wrong?

These are the questions that flooded my heart.

But God began to speak peace, giving me specific instructions, and my relationship with God grew stronger in that season.

Instead of being bitter at God, the Holy Spirit helped me divert my anger to the enemy and convert it to a fuel for me never to give up in life. God created a stronger resolve in my spirit to become a tyrant to the enemy, and to ensure I fulfil my destiny.

That was a determining moment for me, it was my turning point. At that moment, I knew nothing could stop me.

I remember giving a speech during my father's burial, and I spoke passionately, from my heart.

And my simple conclusion was – friends and family had gathered to celebrate, and even though my dad had not left great material wealth and possessions behind for us, he had showed us the priceless path of life. He had given us Jesus and with Him, we would make it through life.

Little did I know that I was speaking prophetically.

This to the glory of God, was a determining moment and a turning point in the life of my family.

God became our Father, and it transformed our lives. And today, we can say 'Indeed, God is faithful'.

It is possible to be restored.

It is possible to be revived.

It is possible for you to come out from a curveball situation that looks impossible. Scripture says in Isiah 43:2; "*When you go through the fire, I will be with you, when you go through the water, you will not be drowned when you go to the fire, I will be with you.*"

God promises that He will be with us. He will not leave us nor forsake us. He is our ever-present help in the time of trouble.

Are you going through a storm right now?

> "*Trust in the Lord with all your heart, lean not to your own understanding. In all your ways acknowledge Him and He will direct your path.*" - ***Proverbs 3:5***

It might be difficult and painful to do this, but remain committed to showing up for your purpose, and shaping up for your dream!

Keep at it, it is not over until you win!

ANCHORED ACTIONS

1. Do you recall a similar challenging time in your life? How did you manage it?

2. What lesson will you never forget about your challenge?

3. Going forward, in what ways will you manage curveballs when they show up in your life?

POINTS TO PONDER

It might be difficult and painful to do this, but remain committed to showing up for your purpose, and shaping up for your dream!

FAITH ALIVE

Dear Brothers and Sisters, when trouble of any kind comes your way, consider it an opportunity for great joy. **- James 1:2-4 (NLT)**

The ability to maintain a positive outward disposition in tribulation is a gift; not everyone can smile through pain.

What helps us to carry on during tribulations is the faith that God knows what we're going through and has given us power to overcome; when things get bad, we have a hope of Glory - Christ.

Keep your faith alive!

When your faith is tested, your endurance has a chance to grow. Therefore, allow your faith to grow. *'For when your endurance is fully developed, you will be perfect, complete, needing nothing'.'* James 1:4

This is an interesting portion of scripture. James 1:22 speaks about *doing the word* and not just being *hearers* alone.

But be ye doers of the word, and not hearers only, deceiving your own selves. For if any be a hearer of the word, and not a doer,

he is like unto a man beholding his natural face in a glass. -
James 1:22-23

One of the ways we can put the word to practise is to intentionally apply it to our lives in every circumstance.

Have you ever tried to be joyful during a challenging situation?

In the book of Job, we read the account of a man called Job whose life was suddenly filled with unpleasant circumstances. What is more interesting about Job is that he responded to his own trials with the attitude of joy. Have you encountered unpleasant situations in your life's journey? How did you respond?

Look at the classic example of our Lord Jesus Christ who came to earth not just to be celebrated, but to pay the ultimate price for the salvation of the world.

The Bible says in Philippians 2:8: *And being found in appearance as a man, He humbled Himself and became obedient to the point of death, even the death of the cross.*

For the joy that was set before Him, Jesus despised the shame and now He is seated at the right hand of God.

It is not easy to rejoice when we are going through tough times, but by the help of the Spirit, we are enabled to tap into the divine and connect to a source of power – to a strength that is beyond us. When we fix our eyes on the One who matters, during challenges, we can find strength to rejoice.

It is natural for you to be sad or depressed when something bad happens. The Bible says there is time for everything – a time to cry, and a time to laugh, but when the enemy expects you to cry and you laugh instead, you are doing something different. You are *laughing in the spirit!*

When you *laugh in the spirit*, not because you are losing your mind or laughing in the flesh, but because you see the God that is beyond anything that you can ever go through; joy becomes a weapon that confounds the enemy.

From the account of Stephen who was being stoned, but still prayed for the people that were killing him, the bible says: *the heavens were opened, and he saw Jesus standing*. Stephen received a standing ovation from heaven.

Situations must never be made a god over our lives, and they must never control or determine the output of our lives, or our thoughts and values. Instead, we must consistently put our faith in our God, and regardless of the season and what we go through, we must continue to look up to the Faithful One that has created us. Our God is ever faithful!

ANCHORED ACTIONS

1. Have you gone through anything that is tough?

2. Have you gone through trials in the past? How did you manage those tough times?

3. Begin to apply the scriptural example of Stephen and ask the Lord to reveal deeper things about the situations you are going through.

POINTS TO PONDER

Situations must never be made a god over our lives, and they must never control or determine the output of our lives, or our thoughts and values. Instead, we must consistently put our faith in our God, and regardless of the season and what we go through, we must continue to look up to the Faithful One that has created us.

DISAPPOINTED

*"In my distress I called to the Lord; I cried to my God for help. From his temple he heard my voice; my cry came before him into his ears." - **Psalm 18:3***

"They can't find a heartbeat!"

It was a cold evening of October 2015.

Purist and I had been married for about four years at the time. I was away at Newcastle where I had a weekend ministration to attend. I had just finished my ministration, and I had been sitting with my hosts at the dinner table of the gala night when I got the call.

Purist's cry of distress at the other end of the line re-echoed in my subconscious.

They can't find a heartbeat!

Dear Lord, not again!

A few hours earlier, I had left Purist in our London home. She was a few weeks pregnant, and that morning she had complained of some spotting, and was going to the hospital to get checked out. But she looked fine.

I prayed with her before I headed out to catch my train to Newcastle. We had believed that everything would work out for good, and we had been very hopeful that this time, this one would stay.

I had never felt so disappointed in my life.

Why, Lord? I asked. Not again!

The first miscarriage had happened within the first few months of our marriage. I was in church on a Sunday morning, Purist had stayed home to rest. I got an emergency call that Purist was in excruciating pain.

I went home immediately and rushed her to the hospital where it was discovered that Purist had an almost ruptured ovarian cyst, and therefore immediate surgery had to be carried out.

It happened so suddenly. One minute I was a happy husband who was leaving his wife at home because she needed to rest, and the next, I was in the waiting room at the hospital, asking God to spare her life and the baby's.

It was turbulent.

I waited there over the night, and in the early hours of the morning, she was brought out of the theatre, and I could finally see her. She looked tired, and drained, and there were monitors attached to her. She had lost one of her tubes, and a few weeks later, we also lost the baby.

That was only the beginning of a series of miscarriages that had happened one after another.

As I sat on that cold floor in Newcastle, it all came back rushing to me.

Why is this happening again?

Eventually, God blessed us with Kairos, and gave us reasons to smile, but we went through a process of wading through disappointments and standing faithfully in God. Our journey is documented in the book: *It's Worth the Wait.*

A disappointment is a feeling of sadness or frustration that is experienced when a negative unexpected event occurs. As a Christian, you will be sure to face tough situations. How do you get the strength to carry on in the face of challenges? How do you deal with disappointments when they come?

When the troubles of life knock at your door, do not be dismayed; look up to Jesus!

May we find the strength to call Him *faithful* even in the face of difficult situations and disappointments.

May we find the strength to not only survive these experiences, but to seek God and get direction for the next level.

May we find the strength in God to live past and rise above disappointments.

ANCHORED ACTIONS

1. Have you experienced disappointment?

2. How do you manage trying and challenging times?

3. Spend some time to think about how your faith has been tried.

POINTS TO PONDER

When the troubles of life knock at your door, do not be dismayed; look up to Jesus!

May we find the strength to call Him *faithful* even in the face of difficult situations and disappointments.

OVERCOMING

*"You… are from God and have overcome them, because the one who is in you is greater than the one who is in the world." - **1 John 4:4***

To overcome means to surmount, prevail over, to get the better of a physical or abstract obstacle. Jesus Christ, our role model, is an overcomer. It is only natural that we too must overcome.

There are several Bible verses where Jesus refers to Himself as an overcomer. John 16:33 says:

"I have told you these things, so that in me you may have peace. In this world you will have trouble. But take heart! I have overcome the world."

Jesus is an overcomer, and as followers of Christ, we are also overcomers, and more than conquerors.

Adversity usually comes unannounced, leaving you with little or no time to leaf through your bible to find an appropriate response. Here are seven steps to overcoming adversity that we must make our safety code. By using these seven steps, you can walk out victoriously out of every situation you face.

STEP 1: Trust

The book of Proverbs chapter 3:5-6 says,

> *Trust in the Lord with all your heart, and lean not on your own understanding, in all your ways acknowledge Him, and He shall direct thy path.*

When you go through difficulty, the most important thing is to trust in the Lord with all your heart. When you are confronted with circumstances that does not make any sense, what's your first response?

You must resist the temptation to be bitter against God.

The natural inclination of man immediately after anything negative happens is to find faults and look for someone to apportion blame to. All this does is give you more reasons to be unhappy, and create more momentum for bitterness, disappointment, and despair.

You find yourself saying things like:

If only this had happened, or
If only this person had been there,
If only this person had helped me…'

These patterns of thought create bitterness, and that is the ultimate plan of the enemy – to steal, kill and destroy, and this starts systematically.

Each time we go through trials, and situations that leave us shaken, we must be ready to put our total trust in the Lord.

It might not make sense to your human mind, but you need to trust God beyond your human understanding and calculation.

STEP 2: Be Thankful:

Another key to overcoming adversity is to give thanks.

The scriptures in I Thessalonians 5:18 encourages us to:

> *"Give thanks in everything for this is the will of God concerning you,"*

How do you give thanks when things are bad?

In an earlier chapter, I spoke about the phone call I received from my sister to inform me of my father's passing.

How do you give thanks when you get such heart-breaking news?

It can only be by the help of the Spirit; immediately you switch into thanksgiving, something happens – God sends His angels to minister to you. I have experienced this.

As you give thanks, you enter the realm of the Divine, exchange your weakness for His strength, and receive inspiration and wisdom. The Lord will begin to reveal deep mysteries to you and give you a peace that passes human understanding.

STEP 3: Be Humble

Humble yourself under the mighty hand of God and He will exalt you. One of the plans of the enemy is to ensure that you stay bitter against God and become disobedient to God's will.

Anytime people are at their lowest, in times of great adversity, they have a feeling like nothing else matters, and there is a natural inclination to pick up self-destructive habits. Usually, they head to the bar to drink, and commit vices, and it is all part of the strategy of the enemy to throw you down that pit of destruction and his endgame is to kill.

In times of adversity, we must stay humble. It takes great humility to put down everything you think you've known or understood about God, and kneel at his feet to say, *Lord, help me*. It takes great humility to do this.

2 Chronicles 7:14 says: ***If my people who are called by my name will humble themselves and pray, I will heal their land (paraphrased).***

While you are trying to make sense of the series of events that an adversity might be unravelling your life, switch to thanksgiving mode, and trust the Lord.

Humble yourself under the mighty hand of God and He will exalt you.

STEP 4: Pray

The bible in James 5:13 says: ***Is any amongst you afflicted? Let him pray***.

Prayer is a place of exchange and communication with God where you trade your weakness for His strength. Prayer is the place where you bring petitions – it is a place where you share your heart desires with God, and where God speaks to you.

The best scripture of all my favourite scriptures is Philippians 4:6 which says, ***"be anxious for nothing but in everything with prayer and supplication with thanksgiving, let your requests be made known."*** The preceding verse says that the peace of God will guard your heart, and this is the aftermath of prayer; the peace of God comes.

I have experienced first-hand, the prayer-answering God. In times of despair and affliction, pray; and the God of peace will pull you out of that troubling situation.

STEP 5: Stay in the Word

The Bible says in 1Samuel 30:6, ***David encouraged himself in the Lord***. You must stay in the Word of God. In Job 32:12b, Job says: *I have esteemed the words of his mouth more than my necessary food.*

You must stay in the Word of God!

When you receive a negative diagnosis, a faith-challenging report or news that is contrary to everything that you have ever believed, you must switch from the human realm of figures and medical sciences, and dive into the Word of God; there you will receive the engrafted Word that can save your soul.

You need to fill your heart with God's truth, which instructs and empowers your faith to receive and birth miracles.

STEP 6: Praise Him

Praise is a powerful weapon. In Psalm 34:1, David says: *"I will bless the Lord at all times and his praise shall continually be in my mouth."*

The bible story tells in Acts 16:25 – in the midst of adversity, and locked up in prison, Paul and Silas began to praise and pray. As a result of this, there was an earthquake, and all the prisoners were loosened from their chains.

There is power in praise!

The scripture is filled with accounts of people who after praising the Lord, experienced the miraculous. Amazing things happen when you truly praise the Lord; whether you are in your room, closet, or in your car while listening to worship music – you can activate the miraculous by praising God.

Praising God will not make sense in relation to the prevalent circumstance, and the enemy will taunt and ask you questions like: *why are you praising God? It does not make any sense to do this!*

Why do you still praise? Have you received the breakthrough? No. So, how can you praise in adversity?

You only praise in adversity when you switch from the natural senses and into the realm of faith, and praise the One that is beyond you; the Alpha and Omega and Creator of the universe, and the One that knew you even before you were in your mother's womb.

Nothing takes Him by surprise. As you praise Him in trust, He pulls you out of your adversity!

STEP 7: Fellowship

The bible says in Hebrews 10:25,

> *"Not forsaking the assembling of ourselves together, as the manner of some is; but exhorting one another: and so much the more, as ye see the day approaching."*

One of the things that the enemy does when people go through trying times is to isolate them for the kill.

Beware of being isolated!

It starts with depression, and a desire for separation. In seasons of adversity, there comes a time when you just want to be alone and be all by yourself. These are times where you are most vulnerable, and prone to make mistakes.

If you are not strong enough on your own, the enemy can attack and take advantage of your weakness, or you can slip into destructive behaviour.

It is important that you remain with other believers, – people who are like minded, and who will encourage you to stay in God.

These are the seven keys to overcoming adversity. Use them to unlock your breakthrough and break free from challenges.

The beauty of overcoming is that you become a champion in the area you might have once struggled through, and God uses your testimony to encourage generations yet unborn, and others who might be going through what you went through.

ANCHORED ACTIONS

A quick recap of the seven steps to overcoming adversity:

STEP 1: Trust

STEP 2: Be Thankful

STEP 3: Be Humble

STEP 4: Pray

STEP 5: Stay in the Word

STEP 6: Praise Him

STEP 7: Fellowship

POINTS TO PONDER

Adversity usually comes unannounced, leaving you with little or no time to leaf through your bible to find an appropriate response.

TESTIFY

"And they overcame him by the blood of the Lamb, and by the word of their testimony..." - revelation 12:11a

Believe it or not, testifying is a way to overcome. Sometimes we get so carried away with living life, and all the things that we are chasing that we do not remember to stop and share God's faithfulness in our lives with others.

We *overcome* when we spread the message of His good news. Within the pages of this book, I have shared several testimonies of what the Lord has done for me; and how He has turned me from nothing to something; the same way in Isaiah 41:14-16, he turned Jacob, whom he described as "a worm", into a threshing instrument.

This is the Lord's doing and it is marvellous in our sight!

The concept of a seed never ceases to fascinate me. How something can grow from *nothing* into *something* is something that repeatedly leaves me in awe.

I have encountered the awesomeness of God, watching Him take me from stage to stage and from glory to glory, despite my weaknesses and shortcomings. I am still a work in progress, and on my journey to becoming all God has created me to be. I consistently see the hand of God in everything that concerns me.

As I look back on my life and all the battles I have fought, and all the things I have gone through, I can see all the great challenges we overcame by the grace of God.

I often think of the past and what God has brought me through – all the times that I struggled, doubted myself, or when Purist and I cried as a couple, on our journey to parenting.

I look at where I am today, and what God is doing in my life currently, and I have reasons to thank Him. God has blessed us with two lovely children Keeona, our daughter, and Kairos, our son, and God has set us on the path to fulfilment of destiny.

All these give me multiple reasons to thank God. We have seen the reward for service, consistency, dedication, and remaining dogged in that which God has called us to do.

Indeed, staying true to your assignment has a reward. The scriptures put it this way in Galatians 6:9 –

> Be not weary in well doing for in due season you will reap if you faint not.

This is the story of my life; this is my testimony.

Looking back at your life, what are the things or stages you have lived through, or God has brought you through?

You have all it takes, and the seed of greatness inside of you; get up and do all that God has called you to!

The world is waiting to hear your testimony!

ANCHORED ACTIONS

1. What are the identifiable things, stages that God has brought you from?

2. How far have you come in the pursuit of purpose?

3. In what ways will you share your testimony to uplift someone else?

POINT TO PONDER

Never stop! Never stop pushing, pressing towards the mark for the price of the high calling. You will win if you do not quit.

"Beyond the norm
Beyond my fears
Beyond the natural
I will excel
I'm soaring high
Beyond the sky
By the power of the
Lord"

Lyrics from Song: Beyond the Norm
Words & Music by Evans Ogboi
©2022 Simplicity Records

ANCHOR 7

EMERGE

"You have everything it takes. There is nothing stopping you now. It is time for you to rise and shine for the glory of God; It is time to emerge!"

- Evans Ogboi

EMERGE

*"You are the light of the world. A city set on a hill cannot be hidden." - **Matthew 5:14(esv)***

To emerge simply means to become visible. It is a decision to take conscious and intentional steps to becoming the best version of yourself.

The understanding that a journey of a thousand miles starts with a step must be ingrained in your subconscious.

We admire great people who have achieved outstanding feats because they put in the work. Until we begin to unleash our own potential and put it to effective use, we will never become effective.

You cannot become effective by analysing the paths to success or comparing yourself to other people.

You start by using what you have, putting it to use, and watching it grow day after day; then you will see the influence God has put on you to spread across the globe.

It is important that we are consistent in our endeavour, purpose or calling. It is your consistency that is rewarded; your decision to not just do it once, but to do it repeatedly.

Consistency is key. You will win if you do not quit. A scripture I love so much in Matthew 7:7 says: *"Keep on asking, and you will receive what you ask for. Keep on seeking, and you will find. Keep on knocking, and the door will be opened to you."*

Always reach out and seek to create value. This is the mind-set of high achievers; and the mind-set that pleases God.

The scripture in Genesis 8:22 says that *"as long as the earth remains, seed time and harvest will never cease."*

This encourages us to continually sow and plant seeds of greatness in people and create value everywhere we go; by doing this, you consistently grow and multiply value. This is a principle that works

As you look back over your journey, you will suddenly realise that you have become effective as your influence begins to grow and spread with the potential that God has given you.

God gave a command in Genesis 1:28:

"Be fruitful, multiply, replenish the earth."

This is the command to fulfil our purpose; replenish the earth, and multiply that which the Lord has put inside you.

You have everything it takes. There is nothing stopping you now. It is time for you to rise and shine for the glory of God; It is time to emerge!

ANCHORED ACTIONS

1. Take time to assess your current level of influence. List at least five of your identified areas of influence.

2. List out five things you will need to keep doing to increase your influence.

POINT TO PONDER

You have everything it takes. There is nothing stopping you now. It is time for you to rise and shine for the glory of God; It is time to emerge!

ACHIEVE

*"Seest thou a man diligent in his business ?" He shall stand before kings..." - **proverbs 22:29***

To become all that God has created us to be, we must build capacity. This means that we must consciously invest in ourselves, strive to be better, at what we do, what we bring to the table, and what we take to the world.

The benchmark for successful achievements is not just in who we become, but what we do and the impact we make. We salt and savour the earth with our gifts, and it is therefore important that we continue to grow and continually build capacity.

To achieve all these, it is important that we constantly resist the temptation to remain in our comfort zone; a challenge that several people face.

Comfort is the number one enemy of your fulfilment and success in life, therefore you must constantly keep breaking out of your comfort places. This means that you should constantly challenge yourself, lift the bar, aim for higher heights across the board, hold yourself to higher standards, and seek to improve and surpass your previous records.

In Proverbs 4:18, the Scripture refers to high achievement this way,

> *"The path of the just shines brighter and brighter until the perfect day."*

When we achieve, we are on the verge of setting the trend and never settling for less; we continually evolve, shine, build capacity, and break out of every mould to break new ground.

As we dedicate ourselves to a life of continual pursuit of purpose, we are bound to succeed in everything that we do.

You will achieve your goals!

You will succeed!

Victory is sure.

ANCHORED ACTIONS

1. Do an evaluation of your current capacity. When was the last time you took on a new course or training?

2. When was the last time you got a promotion or commendation?

3. List out five new skills or learning points you acquired within the past one year.

4. Do you have a personal / career plan for the next three years, five years and ten years? Write them down.

POINT TO PONDER

Comfort is the number one enemy of your fulfilment and success in life, therefore you must constantly keep breaking out of your comfort places.

BRINGING IT HOME

*"Having Done All to Stand, Stand…" - **Ephesians 6:13b***

As we draw to the close of his book, I am excited at what has been activated in your insides, and I cannot wait to hear about your journey, your successes, and your testimonies.

Sharing all of this with you has helped me reinforce my belief in the wisdom and operations of God in my life. He has truly been faithful.

Now, is God done with me? Most certainly not! He is not done with you either!

The scripture in Rom 8:19 tells us that:

The creation is waiting for the manifestation of the sons of God.

There is so much God needs to get done, and you and I have roles to play. You must emerge for God to use you!

God needs willing and credible vessels to do His work and your maturity and level of understanding is important for God to place greatness in your hands.

Remember Joseph went through experiences at the well, as a slave-boy and a prisoner before he finally arrived at the Palace. Greatness can only glide on those experiences.

Our Lord Jesus also walked the walk of shame to be lifted. We all must go through our own process in God's customised dimensions before we emerge!

I trust God that your light will not go out till you finish your race.

You will fulfil destiny!

You will rise!

You will shine!

Men will come to your horizon and be drawn to your light!

You will soar on challenges!

You will not fail!

Together, we shall all finish the race in glory.

ACKNOWLEDGEMENT

In life no good thing is ever achieved by one person. We all require assistance to get to our destination. I must take the time to appreciate some of the men and women God has used in my life thus far.

First, I must thank God for my father, Late Lawrence Emina Ogboi, of blessed memory, who's gone to be with the Lord, for not only bringing me to earth, but nurturing me in the way of the Lord, giving me the foundation that has sustained and helped me develop my own relationship with God; which ultimately led to locating my purpose and assignment.

I also thank God also for my mother, Mrs. Roseline Ogboi. I thank God for her love, ceaseless prayers and support towards helping me discover my innate gift at a very tender age, back in Church of God Mission, Benin City, Nigeria; for allowing me to travel the nation and trusting me as a teenager to head to Lagos, Nigeria and stand on my own. Mom may God bless you for allowing me to become all that God has called me to be.

I want to thank my wife, Purist Ogboi, for being such an inspiration and motivation. She is a huge support and blessing to my destiny. I bless the day that I met you. Thank you for always being the voice of encouragement and allowing me to grow into all that God has ordained me to be. Thank you for being a brilliant loving mother to our beautiful children, Kairos and Keeona. Thank you for being so loving and ever kind. Thank you for being ever humble. Thank you for being such a great helper of destiny.

I want to thank God for all my siblings, and all my in-laws, notably, my father-in-law, Pastor Jonathan Udochukwuka, and my mother-in-law, Pastor Mrs. Mabel Udochukwuka, for bringing such a beautiful gift into this world, and for entrusting their daughter, Purist, into my hand. Thank you for all the love and the ceaseless prayers over the years. Thank you for always being there. I love you so much.

I thank God for Mr. Peter Longe, the gentleman that God used to sow the first seed into my music ministry, to allow me kicks-tart what God would have me do. Thank you, sir, may the heavens remain continually open over you.

I thank God for Pastor Christy, way back in Fountain of Life, Victoria Island Parish, who was a mother that helped me during my formative years, to believe in myself, and grow as a young man.

I want to thank God for Pastor Olumide Olugbenle, the pastor Rehoboth International Christian Centre of (previously Fountain of Life, Victoria Island Parish), for being a bedrock who God used to train me during my formative years in Lagos, Nigeria. We can never offer enough gratitude, sir. God bless you. Pastor Mowunmi Olugbele and the entire house of Rehoboth Community!

I want to thank God for my pastor, the pastor of *RCCG Living Faith Connections*, London, Pastor Chris Adeoye, and my dear mother in the Lord, Pastor Abi Adeoye, for your love and support over the years and for taking me in as a son. It has been an incredible journey working with you in ministry. Thank you!

I want to thank God for my pastor, Pastor Jonathan Oloyede, and Pastor Abby Oloyede – you have always been there at the right time to speak words of life and encouragement, even at the darkest time of our lives. Thank you for being there.

To all my friends, partners in the ministry, and all our family members across the globe, thank you for your love, prayers, and support. This is possible because God used you in one way or the other to be a blessing to me.

Finally, I want to thank the Creator of my soul– my Lord and Saviour Jesus Christ, for allowing me to find purpose, and to find Him at a tender age. Thank you, Lord, for calling me into ministry, and for leading me in the path of life. Thank you for your grace to continually press on for Your will to be done in my life. Thank you for giving me the courage to push despite obstacles, thank you for the grace to recover all. Thank you for the abilities and for every gift you have given to me. May my life continually be to the praise and glory of your name!

Blessed be the Lord God almighty, Father, Son, and the Holy Ghost. Amen!

ABOUT THE BOOK

It's Possible... Believe!

What is that one thing you desire so badly, you wonder if it can ever become a reality?

Are you seeking to clinch that gold medal? Birth an impossible dream? Marry the girl of your dreams? Throw your graduation cap to the blue skies? Break the ceiling of your career? Get a promotion at work? Nurse a dying business to flourishing health? Carry your long-awaited baby in your arms? Walk into a season of breakthrough? Repair a broken relationship?

Friends, I would like to announce to you, that whatever you seek to achieve, it is possible!

Life holds many surprises; the ability to stand firm, remain unshaken, reach for your goals and live your dreams lies within your reach.

In this book, award-winning producer and gospel artiste, **Evans Ogboi** shares seven anchors based on God's word that equip you to fulfil purpose and remain on a steady course when life's winds blow.

Break out of limiting belief systems, shatter ceilings, reach for a life of possibilities, and unlock the greatness that God has deposited in you!

ABOUT THE AUTHOR

Evans Ogboi is a gifted singer, songwriter, music producer, recording artist and author. He is the music director of the award-winning *Living Faith Connections* Mass Choir in London, UK. He is also a trained sound engineer from SAE institute London, SAE is known as the leading creative media institute worldwide.

Evans is the CEO *Simplicity Records* and has produced several artistes including UK-based gospel artistes Purist Ogboi, Isabella and Kome UDU, to mention a few.

He is the recipient of several awards including: 2014 MOBO Award for Best Gospel Act; 2016 JUMP MVA; and 2018 AGMMA Male Artiste of Excellence, Europe.

He has released three albums and numerous singles, and hosts *Synergy*, an annual event that brings artistes from around the world together, to celebrate Jesus.

With over 21 years of service in church ministry, Evans continues to serve alongside his wife, Purist Ogboi, and is committed to inspiring people with his story and experience.

When you experience more than you can bear, it takes
Love, **Hope** and **Strength** to keep you sane…

IT'S WORTH THE WAIT

By Evans & Purist Ogboi

Life is beautiful and rosy until tragedy strikes. Not once. Not twice. But four times!

Will their faith in God and their love for each other be strong enough to pull them through the test and trials that life throws at them?

It's Worth the Wait is a first-hand narration written by **Evans and Purist Ogboi**, and it chronicles the origin of their love for music, God, and each other.

Printed in Great Britain
by Amazon